GOD-SHAPED VOID

Adam Spencer

God-Shaped Void
ISBN 978-1-7348837-1-8

Copyright @ 2020 by Adam Bryant Spencer
All rights reserved. No part of this publication
may be reproduced or transmitted in any form
without prior written permission from the author.

DEDICATION:

*This book is dedicated to my children
Savannah, Addie, Mikey, Dayla and Samuel.
May you always marvel at the breath of life and
the art in each day. The sun rises and sets with you.
I am so lucky to be your Dad.*

ACKNOWLEDGEMENTS:

Special thanks to my friends who encouraged me to spew my thoughts on paper: Kip Smith, Matt & Veronica Crotta, Doug Richner, Robert Day, Claudia Fletcher, Mike Kelley and Tom Bradwell — without you there would be no book. Thank you to Tess Stockslager for editing the first draft. Thanks to Blair Marketing team and Kip Smith for your expertise. Thank you to my parents for their faithful prayers and my brothers Mark & Matt for your support. Thank you to my beautiful wife, Erica, for listening to me for hours talk about the meaning of life and being so supportive. Most of all, thank you to my Creator. You push me to be better, to live authentically as You repurpose the broken pieces into a beautiful mosaic. May You be glorified.

TABLE OF **CONTENTS**

Introduction — 7

1: Pursuing Fulfillment — 10

2: Our Core Decision-Making — 16

3: The Pleasure-Driven Life or Power-Driven Life — 19

4: The Promise- or Premise-Driven Life — 26

5: The Passion-Driven Life — 32

6: The Purpose-Driven Life — 38

7: A Journey Back to Our Roots — 45

8: The Fifth Core Influencer — 53

9: Filling My Void in Every Area of My Life — 66

10: Strategic Pause — 79

11: Relationship, not Religion — 88

12: Grace, not Legalism — 94

13: Living the Life You Were Created For — 100

Introduction

What is the meaning of life? Why do I exist? Does God have a plan for me? We have all asked those or similar questions.

There is indeed a *purpose* for our existence. We are here on earth by design, not by default. **But what if at the core there was a greater question?** Yes, a greater question than what our *purpose* is, something deeper in our core, the true answer to the groans of humanity. The painful reality is that **you and I could fulfill our purpose 100% and still be carrying a massive God-size-void,** still empty and longing to be filled.

Sadly, *purpose* is where most self-help books and even Christian living books will leave readers off on their journey of hope and healing, because until now we (yes, even those of us in the evangelical Christian community at large) have believed that *purpose* is the ultimate solution to filling our void. We live off of Band-Aid statements like, "God has a plan for your life" or "You can do anything you set your mind to it". And we become obsessively self-absorbed in our search for significance in our daily lives. Yet, if living a *purposeful* life (or the familiar "purpose-driven" life) was the key to fulfillment, why are suicide, depression, obesity, debt, divorce, addictions, poverty and crime each at such unprecedented levels today, in both religious and secular societies?

Millions of people fulfill what they consider their *purpose* in their education, in their careers, in their relationships and even in their religious pursuits, and yet they still find themselves *void* of fulfillment.

Perhaps that is you? You're reading this book because you've reached your goals, you've established healthy relationships, you've celebrated successes, you've reached the pinnacle of your dreams, you're tenured in your religious faith and yet a *void* remains.

Maybe you haven't been so lucky. Instead, your life's

Introduction

journey has been detoured by fractured relationships, a devastating diagnosis, lost opportunities, failed endeavors, shattered dreams or a natural calamity. In your brokenness or uncertainty, you question how your present circumstances fit with God's *purpose* for your life.

Dear reader, your quest for the meaning of life is about to take you to a place of understanding and clarity that will transform everything in your life, great and small, and finally lead you to *filling your void.*

PURSUING **FULFILLMENT**

What is the meaning of life? Why am I here? We have all asked these two questions. What we really want to know is, do I have value and do I matter? From a young age we are set on this course of discovering our purpose, our identity. We ask the young child, "What do you want to be when you grow up?" When they graduate we encourage them with words like, "Be all you can be," or "Follow your dreams." We assume that somehow if we just fulfill what we believe is the *purpose* for our lives we will find fulfillment. If we've married the right person or not. If we've advanced far enough in our career or not. If we've lost enough weight or not. If we've parented well enough or not. If we've saved enough money or not. And yet even after we've made the right choices and achieved our set goals, for many of us there still lingers a *void* in our lives. For some of us the *void* is like a small murmur of unrest that we just can't seem to shake. We've hid it well, and even convinced ourselves it doesn't matter as we chase distractions to numb the pain. For others the *void* is more ominous, like a heavy weight restricting us from the fulfilling life we long for.

To fill the *void* within us, we often try to reinvent ourselves in an alternate reality of who we want people to see us as, forever tweeting, posting, snapchatting, posturing and repositioning ourselves to appear we are happy and truly living a life of fulfillment. But it's all so exhausting! Isn't it? We double down on our responsibilities, become even more driven in our careers, in our weight loss or whatever activity we can, in hopes that the *purpose* that defines us may fulfill us, but it doesn't. We intensely play, recklessly eat, carelessly spend money, and even excessively sleep to feed the aching of this inner void. But it only temporarily helps.

Many of us become so desperate to fill the *void* that we are willing to cheat or live double lives to fill our *void* and achieve the *purpose* that drives us to success, even if it means hiding a lie. We see this played out on the news with the latest celebrity, athlete, politician, preacher, who falls from grace. Their desperate and often reckless pursuit of filling the *void* leads to catastrophic results that hurt themselves and those around them.

You and I would never do that! Right? Or would we? How far would you or I go to fill *our* void? Perhaps the only real difference between us and these infamous people is that our void hasn't been exposed yet. And perhaps you're saying, "I'll never cheat my way to finding fulfillment in my life." The reality is, even if we're not cheating others, we may be cheating ourselves! Yes, cheating ourselves out of *a life free of void*. It's why this book has been written. I don't want anyone to settle for less than the full meaning of life. I want every person to discover how the void in their life can be filled, no matter how great or small it is.

We are each here on earth not by default, but by

design. Which means there is a source and solution to experience life to its fullest. I invite you to join me on a journey of a discovery that changes everything! Discover the *meaning of your* life and *fill your void.*

Points to Ponder:

- *In what areas in your life do you feel weighed down, empty, or conflicted?*

- *In what ways have you tried to address those areas successfully or unsuccessfully?*

NOTES:

2

OUR CORE **DECISION-MAKING**

"Follow your heart!"

"Go with your gut!"

"Listen to your body!"

"Channel your mind!"

We have all received or given advice like that, right? So which do I follow? Is it my heart, gut, body, or mind?

At the core of each of our lives there is something that drives us, something that motivates us. Our core is where we form all our decisions. What we choose to be at the core impacts everything! Every area of our life, great and small, is affected by our *core*. Having the wrong thing at the core can result in living unfulfilled, with an emptiness that can cause a cavernous *void*

OUR CORE DECISION-MAKING

that decays our joy and well-being. This void can even become deadly.

In this book, we will refer to the *source* of our decision-making as the *core*.

There are five layers of every person's *core* decision-making. Every decision in your life is generated by one or more of these five *core influencers*. Every decision, great or small. Regardless of your values, gender, race, education level, or age, every single decision a person makes is generated from one of these five influencers of our core.

Think of these core influencers like five rings layered inside of each other. The external ring or surface ring is our most impulsive influencer. The deeper the layers, the more mature and introspective our core influencers are. The goal is to develop the discipline to channel every decision from the innermost layer of the core of our heart, while still giving value to the other four layers.

However, this discipline is worthless if the wrong thing is at the center of our core. Most of us function daily utilizing only the first four layers/influencers.

What is missing at the center of our core—the fifth layer and innermost influencer—is the key to *filling the void* that is hidden in each of us.

By unlocking the fifth and innermost layer of your heart's core, you will transform how you see yourself, how you make decisions, how you view others, and most of all how you will live each day to the fullest meaning of life.

3

THE **PLEASURE-DRIVEN** LIFE OR **POWER-DRIVEN** LIFE

As stated in the previous chapter, there are five layers of every person's *core* decision making. Every decision in your life is generated by one or more of these five *core influencers*. Before we discover what's missing at the center of our core, let's quickly define each of the outer four layers.

The first core influencer and the most external layer is *pleasure* and *power*. If we only had this one layer of influence, we might make every decision based on feelings. Does it make me happy? Is it desirable? Does it feed my appetite for *pleasure*? The opposite can apply, leading us to say "no" because something doesn't taste good, feel good, or entertain us enough. There doesn't need to be any rationale here, or depth of responsibility, or pause for considering cause and effect of the choice at hand.

The *pleasure*-driven decision making influencer is the first one we learn after we are born. A newborn baby with distressful tears and agonized cries immediately finds fulfillment from a nipple producing milk.

A decision made that is only influenced by *pleasure* does not require rationale or much forethought. *Pleasure*-driven choices are often impulsive: leave a child unattended with a large, open bag of Skittles, and chances are you will find them moments later with colorful sticky fingers, followed by a tummy ache. Accessible doesn't mean permissible. But a person driven solely by *pleasure* doesn't care if something is permissible. They only care if it is accessible and momentarily satisfies the cravings of their *void*.

Making choices that produce pleasurable results is not a bad thing. In fact, as we will learn in the chapters ahead, *pleasure* is a key ingredient to the composite of a meaningful life.

In its rightful order of influence, *pleasure* prompts the internal questions: Does this option appeal to me, does it taste good, does it feel good, do I enjoy it? These are natural and appropriate questions. However, the danger is making all our decisions, great and small, **solely** on whether the outcome is *pleasurable.*

Our sexualized culture gives license for *pleasure-*driven relationships that lack commitment and exclusivity—two pillars of mature love. As a result, relationships founded on *pleasure* alone, never last.

Imagine a life where the only choices I made were the ones that were *pleasurable*: to eat and drink whatever I craved, to have sex with whomever I pleased, to consume whatever pleased me, to buy whatever I wanted, without any consideration of potential negative consequences.

It's easy to see how this kind of lifestyle can get out of hand and lead to a life devoid of sustainable satisfaction.

Sharing this outer layer of our core, closely aligned with *pleasure*, is the core influencer of *power.*

The *power*-driven life is motivated by the question of what fuels a person's appetite for independence, control, and influence. Maximizing the power of your own influence can enhance personal outcomes in your life, and moreover the lives of those you come into contact with.

Just like *pleasure*, we learn the influencer of power at a very young age.

The toddler learns to crawl, stand, then walk as a result of this innate desire for *power* or independence. As parents we balance their growth with age-appropriate boundaries, often causing resistance at bedtime, perhaps even a meltdown or temper-tantrum from the parental barrier of "no."

Later as emerging adults, our teenagers are empowered to make independent choices, while as parents we expand or release boundaries.

In the workforce, we study, train, and gain the necessary experience to develop the *power* to have greater impact in our trade.

Power is a natural progression of maturation for every person, student, professional. However, power without compassion or accountability is reckless.

Imagine a person whose every decision is influenced **solely** by *power* and *pleasure*. We can easily see how lethal this kind of life can be, and how it can lead to an abuse of *power*.

The priest who leverages his authoritative position to sexually abuse children for decades, for example. The scores of high-profile men in *powerful* positions whose careers and reputations have been shattered by the unveiling of years of hidden sexual harassment of women, which has spawned the "Me Too Movement," is another example of how lethal a *power* and *pleasure*-driven life can be.

Does this mean that *power* and *pleasure* are wrong or that we shouldn't seek them? Absolutely not. But they cannot be at the center *core* of our decision-making.

The warning here is that if *pleasure* and *power* are all that motivate our every decision, we will be self-consumed—to our own detriment and to the detriment of those around us.

And ultimately our life will be *void* of true fulfillment.

Points to Ponder:

- *In what areas of our culture do you see people living a pleasure-driven life?*

- *In what areas of our culture do you see abuse of power?*

- *What pleasure-driven decisions have you made in your life that you regret?*

- *What examples in your own life can you think of where someone used their power (or influence) in a way that negatively impacted you?*

NOTES:

4

THE **PROMISE-** OR **PREMISE-DRIVEN** LIFE

This is where we start to see some depth in the layers of our core. Our decision is no longer coming from the surface alone. There is a predicated motivation that causes us to pause before we make our decision. Here we may even make a choice that we don't like or want to because we are influenced by a *promise* or *premise*.

The child pauses before disobeying his parents because he was promised a consequence.

She stayed in an abusive relationship because, "He promised he would never hit me again."

"I never wanted to be in the Army, but I always felt there was a *premise* that because my father and my grandfather and my brothers all served in the military, it was expected of me as well," the middle-aged man said.

Promises and *premises* are not all bad. When Dave's marriage was tough and that opportunity for an affair came along, he chose not to because he remembered his vows and the *promise* he made to his spouse.

Nancy believed the *premise* that if she studied hard or learned a trade she would have a better chance at a successful career.

Children survive the fear of the first day of kindergarten because they had the *promise* from their parent(s) that they will return at the end of the day to pick them up.

"Swing me Daddy, swing me!" My little girl pleaded. Both of our arms stretched out, connected only by our hands, Savannah floats through the air as I swing her in a waist-high circle, faster and faster. Her exuberant request is repeated every 90 seconds with the *premise* that I won't let her go, and she is always safe with her daddy.

There was a *premise* when you took the job that you would have opportunities for advancement if you worked hard enough. There is a *promise* that your workplace would be free of sexual harassment.

When the flight took off the passengers had a *premise* that the airplane was safe. The used car salesman *promised* you a great deal.

Every day our lives are impacted by healthy *premises* and *promises*.

But what happens when *promises* are broken and *premises* are unfounded? If we have made these influencers **alone** the core of our decision making, we will ultimately find ourselves *void* of fulfillment. Why? Because we are imperfect people living in a broken world. Strangers, people in authority, even the people that are close to us will fail or disappoint us. We will even fail ourselves. Have you ever broken a *promise* you made to yourself? Have you ever forgotten the *premise* of a situation that led to an unsatisfactory outcome? Diets come and go, relationships struggle, addictions resume, finances fluctuate, because hardship can stop at anyone's door without warning.

Even a marriage based on a *promise* made at the altar and the *premise* that he/she will never leave no matter what, is often a license for a spouse to take advantage of the other person. He knew she would never leave him, so he cheated on her anyway. The *premises* that "we were high-school sweethearts" and "we know we'll grow old together" are faulty foundations. A marriage or any healthy partnership must have more than the layers of *promise/premise* and *pleasure/power* to survive.

A fulfilled life requires decisions based on more than *pleasure, power, premise,* and *promises.*

Points to Ponder:

- *What are some premises that you once held that turned out to be false?*

- *What current premises are most important to you?*

- *What promises have most influenced your life?*

- *What broken promises have contributed the most to your void?*

NOTES:

THE **PASSION-DRIVEN** LIFE

The third layer of our core is *passion*. It is the most commonly used layer of our decision-making. Without a strong center at our core, most of our right or wrong decisions are generated from this third layer. *Passion* is emotionally charged. It can in the moment trump all logic. It allows us to conquer our fears. It gives breath to imagination. It drives with unpredictable pace. It knows no boundaries. It overtakes reason and breaks down barriers of all sizes. *Passion* is the fire that ignites change. A life without *passion* is a sterile life. *Passion* opens the door to compassion, conviction, imagination, and determination.

The child's imagination gives birth to their *passions*.

Many teachers, doctors, and successful professionals can trace their career choice back to the early onset of a *passion* for their field as a young child.

I live in a college town with both sacred and secular universities. I enjoy going to local coffee shops and hearing students talk with such conviction about their *passions*. They are convinced that they are going to cure cancer, feed a million orphans, create an app that predicts the future, and build an elevator to the moon. They don't realize that before they can attempt to fulfill these *passionate* dreams, they will most likely have to work a typical 9-5 job for several years to pay off their student loans before the door to their dreams appears—if the dream is still alive by then. Yet some of our greatest startups, inventions, and innovations are coming from millennials. So, to throw water on the flames of their passion would be the worst thing we could do. But there should be a balance, right? There is more to making an informed decision than just *passion*.

The truth is, we can be *passionately* wrong. Have you ever met someone like this? They speak with such conviction. They possess unwavering grit. Their charisma is contagious. They have tunnel vision on their goal, and there is no convincing them otherwise. They are driven by a passion of reckless abandonment. They are all in, sold out to their passion. But does that make them right?

Consider the contestant on a TV talent show who is deeply *passionate* about singing (so much so they've convinced themselves they have the talent to win and become a star). Seconds into their audition, they are booed and/or dismissed. Their *passion* quickly sours to depression or denial, and the *void* they tried so desperately to fill with their *passion* has only grown more ominous.

A *pleasure/power-*, *promise/premise-*, and *passion-driven-life* alone only leads to a life *void* of the fulfillment you and I long for.

You took that job with the *premise* you'd be good at it. You were *promised* a fair wage, you find *pleasure* in some of your essential work tasks, you have *power* to influence outcomes of your work, and you are *passionate* about the mission and vision of your employer, but... something is missing.

Or perhaps you're in a relationship under the *premise* that it's true love. Your partner *promised* to have eyes for you only. You enjoy the *pleasure* of exclusive intimacy. You have *power* to influence your partner's agenda as you jointly build your relationship. You're *passionately* in love with your partner. And yet, something is missing, or something has gone wrong or unexpected, and you need to make a decision that will affect everything, so you need a deeper influence.

A life with decisions led by *passion* alone will lead to burnout, disappointment and an existence *void* of fulfillment. There is something more important to have at our core decision-making.

Points to Ponder:

- *What are you most passionate about?*
- *When have your passions led you to a place or decision you later regretted?*

NOTES:

THE **PURPOSE-DRIVEN** LIFE

The fourth inner layer of decision making and moving closer to our core is *purpose*. Of the first four layers, this is the most mature influencer. A *purpose*-driven decision evaluates elements such as motive and potential outcomes. A *purpose*-driven life is healthy because it prompts questioning before responding rather than simply reacting. If we are *purposeful* in our decision making we will be less impulsive. Therefore, our decisions will be more informed and, we hope, produce better outcomes. Just like *pleasure/power*, *premise/promise*, and *passion*, *purpose* is also innate within us.

It speaks directly to the question of the meaning of life, why am I here, what is my *purpose*?

THE PURPOSE-DRIVEN LIFE

As children mature, so does their quest for discovering *purpose* in all facets of life. "Why do I have to go to bed so early, Daddy?"; "Why are there so many stars in the sky, Mommy?"; "Do I have to get a shot at the doctor's office today?"; "Why don't penguins fly?"; "What are belly-buttons for?" These innocent questions evoke a curiosity within us. The more we understand about life, the more we seek to find our *purpose* in every situation.

Throughout our lives, we will make many *purposeful* choices in hopes of having a life of fulfillment. Where to go to college, whom to marry, which jobs to choose. Even our small choices have *purpose*: what we eat, what we wear, the words we choose to speak.

So it makes sense to live a *purpose*-driven life. A life without *purpose* is a life without meaning. It's why that questions haunts so many of us: "What's my *purpose*?" It's one of the most talked-about questions in sacred and secular settings.

Several years ago, author Rick Warren wrote a book by the same title that became a *New York Times* bestseller, with over 25 million copies sold worldwide.

GOD-SHAPED VOID

It was the fastest-selling and greatest-selling Christian living book of all time, other than the Bible. It seems people are really wanting to know how to live a *purpose-driven* life. And it makes sense, right? "What is God's plan for my life?"; "What am I here on earth for?" These are some of the most persistent questions throughout human history.

However, the sad reality is that you and I could fulfill our purpose 100% and still be carrying a massive God-size-void, still empty and longing to be filled.

The truth is, each of us is here by design, not by default. There is indeed a *purpose* for our existence. **But what if at the core there was a greater question?** Yes, a greater question than what our *purpose* is, something deeper in our core, the true answer to the groans of humanity.

Sadly, *purpose* is where most self-help books and even Christian living books will leave readers off on their journey of hope and healing, because until now we have believed that *purpose* is the ultimate solution to our void. "God has a plan for your life." That is our Band-Aid answer for everything. Yet, if living a *purposeful* life (or purpose-driven life) was the key to fulfillment, why are suicide, depression, obesity, debt, divorce, addictions, and crime, each at such unprecedented levels today, in both religious and secular societies?

Millions of people fulfill their *purpose* in their education, in their careers, in their relationships and even in their religious pursuits, and yet they still find themselves *void* of fulfillment.

Perhaps that is you? You're reading this book because you've reached your goals, you've established healthy relationships, you've celebrated successes, you've reached the pinnacle of your dreams, you may even be established in your religious faith, and yet a *void* remains.

Or maybe you haven't been so lucky. Instead, your life's journey has been detoured by fractured relationships, a devastating diagnosis, lost opportunities, failed endeavors, shattered dreams or a natural calamity. In your brokenness or uncertainty, you question how your present circumstances fit with God's *purpose* for your life.

For each of us, filling our *void* requires more than *pleasure* and *power, premise* and *promises, passion,* and *purpose.* There is something more important than all the above influencers, and without this something, the other four influencers are rendered pointless.

The missing influencer is the innermost foundation at the center of our core, the bullseye for which we should target the start of each decision-making process. This fifth influencer gives breath to our *purpose*. Our purpose is what we are *passionate* about. What we are *passionate* about becomes the *premise* of our daily lives. It is ultimately what produces true *pleasure* and enables us to have *power* of influence over every single decision we make.

Dear reader, your quest for the meaning of life is about to take you a place of understanding and clarity that will transform everything in your life great and small and finally lead you to *filling your void.*

Points to Ponder:

- *How would you describe the void in your life?*
- *How long have you had this void?*
- *How have you tried to fill the void?*
- *What would you guess is the fifth and innermost layer of your core? Hint: it also starts with the letter "P."*

NOTES:

7

A JOURNEY
BACK TO OUR ROOTS

To find this missing influencer of our core, we have to travel back in time to our roots, to a garden called Eden. There we will discover the hidden essence of our *void*. If you are an atheist or not yet a subscriber to the Christian faith, I encourage you to read on. There is a practical application for you, too, that will change everything!

For the practicing Christian I warn you: what you are about to discover will rock you to your *core* and change everything you thought you built your faith upon. Regardless of your race, religion, gender, the fifth and greatest influencer you're about to discover can **fill your** *Void* and equip you to live the life you were created for.

GOD-SHAPED VOID

I remember as a young daddy, coming home from work, and hearing the padding of little feet racing down the hallway, as I opened the front door. "Daddy, Daddy, Daddy, Daddy's home!" my little knee-high boy screeched with excitement every day without fail. Samuel's little eyes were fixed on the window, waiting for my arrival. I could hear his excitement as I walked down the sidewalk and up the front steps. I treasured those daily homecomings. No matter what challenges came with the day, it all was erased by the anticipation we both shared for our reuniting. There was something magical about the bond my son and I have shared. He is a teenager now, and yet even at the age of 15, every morning when he wakes up the very first thing he does is find me and give me a hug. I am so grateful for this unbreakable bond we share as father and son.

The book of Genesis paints a similar picture. After God had created the earth and the animals, out of dust he created the first human beings: Adam and Eve. We learn that "in the cool of the day" (Genesis 3:8) God would walk with Adam & Eve, His beloved children. It's an incredible picture. Adam and Eve spending the day roaming the wilderness experiencing the splendor of all God had created, then concluding their daily adventures with fellowship with their Heavenly Father. It must have been around 6:30 in the evening. Perhaps in a valley lush with trees there was a rock established as their meeting spot. And through a small clearing at the top of a knoll their eyes search for Him. "Is He here yet, Eve?" Adam asks. "Shhh, Adam, I think I hear something." A pause. Nope, just a giraffe. Like children giddy to see their daddy, they can hardly contain their excitement when suddenly they see Him appear at the top of a knoll then walking towards them. Unable to wait a moment longer, they burst from their meeting spot and race towards Him, both leaping into His arms as He meets them halfway, with a smile only a father can give. "God, today was amazing! We saw these animals with horns on their heads and we named them elephants," Adam blurts out. And before he could finish, Eve jubilantly recounts the moment she dunked Adam's head under the water.

You can just imagine stories like this being offered up day after day with their Creator, their God, their

Heavenly Father. And we can picture the love He must have felt to receive from His beloved children whom He created. Under their own free will, such perfect love was abounding...until...

My son Samuel was a curious four-year-old mesmerized by the toy aisle. Distracted for a moment, I turned back only to find him no longer standing in the aisle next to me. My heart sank. Perhaps if you're a parent you've experienced the same heartsick feeling. I sprinted down the aisle, then to the next, and the next, all the while in a panicked voice shouting, "Samuel, Samuel, Samuel." But no response. My chest tightened, my face flushed, tears streaming down my cheeks. "Samuel, Samuel, Sammmuueelll." Minutes felt like an eternity, as the worst possible scenarios played in my mind....

Genesis reveals a similar stunning account: In chapter three, we read the most heartbreaking, gut-wrenching scene in all of human history.

The breeze shifts into the "cool of the day," and just like previous days, God the Heavenly Father walks over the knoll, through the valley towards the meeting spot. But on this day, something is different. No one is running toward Him. He walks closer and begins to call out their names. But there is no answer. As He reaches their chosen meeting spot, He calls out again, louder, yet still no answer. And there in that moment we hear the deepest and saddest three words ever uttered in human history. With His heart shattered, He cries out, "Where are you?"

In that very moment, a *void* was created between the heart of God and *all* of humanity. A massive separation fracturing a union that was perfect into a chasm of despair. This same God-shaped void exists in each of us today. How do we know? Because God is still asking the same question that He asked in the Garden of Eden. He is asking you, dear reader, "Where are *you*?"

YOU are His beloved. You've been created in His image. You are not here by default. You are here by design. And He desperately desires a relationship with you! The depth of the love He has for you is unmeasurable. Before you were even born He knew you. (Jeremiah 1:5) He desires to fill the *void* in your life, if only you will let Him. He wants to restore the relationship that was broken in the Garden of Eden. In order to do that, we need to understand what was **lost** when the *void* occurred, and what our responsibility is in response.

Points to Ponder:

- *How does it feel to know that God has been in pursuit of you for your entire life?*

- *Have there been moments in your life that you felt the nudging, whispers or hand prints of God in your life? Describe those moments here:*

NOTES:

THE FIFTH **CORE INFLUENCER**

The God-shaped void entered human history on that fateful day in the Garden of Eden. Every human being since then has been born with the effects of that God-shaped *void* in our hearts. We've tried to fill the *void* with sex, power, religion, money, war, materialism, medicine, and endless other futile efforts. And yet the *void* remains. When the *void* occurred, something was lost that day. That thing that was lost is the fifth core influencer, the most important layer of our decision making, the key to filling our *void*. Genesis reveals it so clearly, and yet we either have missed it or have chosen to ignore it.

They could hear the anguish in God their Father's voice, growing louder and louder as they hid in the bushes nearby. A few hours earlier, Adam and Eve had disobeyed the only rule their Heavenly Father had given them. He told them they could go wherever and have whatever they wanted as long as they didn't eat from a specific tree in the Garden. Nonetheless, they were tempted by a fallen angel named Lucifer who appeared to them in the form of a snake. He convinced them to trust him instead of trusting their Heavenly Father. Eve, then Adam, ate a piece of fruit from the forbidden tree. (Genesis 3:1-6) Immediately they became aware of their lethal mistake. Adam and Eve knew they had disobeyed God, and therefore they clothed themselves with leaves and hid from Him. And here lies the greatest missed observation of the modern day Christian church. It is the fifth and innermost influencer of our core. It is the answer to this question: *What did Adam and Eve lose when they disobeyed God?*

Pleasure? No, despite their disobedience and the changes it brought, they still had each other and the abundance of creation.

Power? No, they had the power to procreate and

have dominion over all the animals.

Promise? God never broke His promises to them.

Premise? They remained His beloved.

Passion? They still wanted to have God's love, even after they disobeyed Him, causing this void.

Purpose? Even after they were punished and banned from the Garden of Eden by God, they were still physically alive and still had access to God.

So, what did they lose when they disobeyed God?

What they lost that day in the Garden thousands of years ago, caused a void that exists in every human being ever to walk the earth since then. Adam and Eve forfeited their *purity*.

Purity is what was lost in the Garden when humanity disobeyed God. **A *purity*-driven life is the only thing that can fill the *God-shaped Void*.** We have a fancy word for *purity* in the Christian religion; it's called righteousness, simply translated, "right-living."

Because of Adam and Eve's disobedience, all of humanity is separated from God. Yet because of our Heavenly Father's immense love for us (His beloved), He set in motion a plan to restore what was lost in the

Garden, by coming to earth in the flesh in the form of a baby. God birthed through a teenage virgin girl His very own Son, named Jesus, to one day become the Savior of humanity, to sacrifice His own life to take our punishment – just to fill the *void* and restore what was lost in the Garden. (Matthew 1:21)

Pause and think about that concept for a moment. God created mankind. Mankind disobeyed God. At that point He could have destroyed the earth. He could have turned His back on humanity forever and left us to our own despair. Instead He sent His own Son, His only Son, to earth to pay the penalty for our (humanity's) disobedience (2 Corinthians 5:21).

During His estimated 33 years on earth, God's Son lived a life of humility, compassion, and mission. Though tempted with the same impurities you and I are faced with daily, Jesus never disobeyed God. Instead, He lived a life of perfection unlike any other person before, during or since. And to fulfill his mission on earth, His Father allowed Him to be wrongfully accused of crimes He did not commit, which led to the imprisonment, torture, and death of Jesus. (Philippians 2:8)

This is where the Easter story unfolds. Jesus, who was 100% human, was also 100% Divine; possessing all the powers of God the Father. And yet He never defended Himself against His accusers. Instead He willingly sacrificed Himself as a substitute for the impurities of humanity. He paid the penalty of humanity's disobedience. His blood shed on the cross (the instrument of His execution) is what cleansed our impurities and forgives us of the debt of our *void*. It is through Jesus and the acceptance of this matchless gift of forgiveness that we can have a restored access to God our Heavenly Father, and ultimately have the resources at our core to fill our *void*. (1 Corinthians 15:3-4)

What Adam and Eve lost is what God sent His son Jesus to restore. It is the whole point of the redemption story of humanity. **God did not send His son Jesus into the world to be tortured and die on a cross to give you and me *purpose*, or *passion*, or *power* or *pleasure*. He sent a Savior to pay the ultimate sacrifice to restore our *purity*.** He brought light into darkness, so that we might see. "Blessed are the *pure* in heart, for they shall see God." (Matthew 5:8)

We often talk about the *passion* of Christ. We know His *purpose*. We read His *promises* in the Bible. We understand the *premises* that He is God's Son and that we are an imperfect people living in a broken world in need of a Savior. We experience the *power* of God in our lives. We can have the *pleasure* (joy) of the Lord as our strength. He represents all of these core influencers. And yet the most important influencer at the core of Jesus's life is His *purity*. Imagine if Jesus wasn't born of a virgin. (Luke 1:26-35) What if He hadn't lived a perfect life? (Hebrews 7:26) What if He didn't ascend into Heaven after His death and resurrection? (Mark 16:19) What if He wasn't *pure*? (1 Peter 2:22) None of this would be possible. Without *purity* His purpose would have been forfeited.

The sacrifice that was needed to restore our relationship with a Holy God required a perfect and *purity*-driven Savior. The blood shed for you and me on the cross is meant to cleanse us from all impurities. Without that cleansing, our *purpose, passions, promises,* and *pleasures* are meaningless and self-serving.

We cannot successfully *fill the void* in our life and

have a relationship with God until we do a ***deep cleanse.***

"Blessed are the pure in heart, for they shall see God" (Matthew 5:8). The original Greek word for pure, used here, is *Kathraros*, from which are derived the English words *cathartic* and *catharsis*. One is a **cleansing agent** to purge the body of impurities. The other is a method of cleansing the mind of such bottled-up feelings as anger and guilt. To be *pure* is to be morally and spiritually clean, and the Holy Spirit is the instrument God uses to deep-cleanse and *purify* us.

The deep cleanse has five simple, yet mandatory steps:

1. First, we must *recognize* that the cause of the *void* in our lives is our separation from God, because of our impurities and mistakes. Even though you and I were not present in the Garden when Adam and Eve chose to disobey God, ever since then, we've been wired to disobey. We are born with this heritage of disobedience. Our human nature, left unchanged, positions us to experience eternal separation from God.

2. Secondly, this deep cleanse requires us to *believe* that only a *pure* and perfect Savior could pay this penalty of our mistakes, on the cross, and provide us restoration and access to a Holy God.

3. *Understand* that this is a free gift that we don't deserve, and we also can never earn it or repay it. Imagine being sentenced to death for a crime you committed...and seconds before your execution, someone steps in and takes your place. There is nothing you could ever do to repay that person. Even if you lived the best life possible to honor that person, it would still never be equal to the sacrifice made on your behalf. That is what Jesus did for you and me. He paid the penalty that we deserved and was our substitute on the cross of execution.

4. Thirdly, the deep cleanse requires us to *ask* God to *forgive* the impure choices

we've made and ask Him to *cleanse* our heart, *cleanse* our mind, and *cleanse* our body.

5. Fourth, *Invite* Him to fill the void in your life with His presence and *remain* the core *influencer* of your heart.

Recognize – Believe – Understand – Ask – Invite

What do steps 4 and 5 look like? How do I "ask" and "invite" God if I can't see Him? What does this "restored access to God" look like? And how do we access these resources? We can't physically walk with God our Heavenly Father. Nor is Jesus physically walking this earth. In the place of His flesh, He abides in us through His Spirit. This Spirit essence is omnipresent, accessible from anywhere at any time. When Jesus physically died on the cross to pay the penalty for humanity's *void*, the restoration plan did not stop there. Easter happened. Three days after Jesus's body was removed from the wooden instrument of his execution and was wrapped in a cloth and placed in a tomb, Jesus came back to life and literally walked out of the tomb. He was seen by many people before He ascended into heaven. In His place, God provided an essence of His likeness that is called the Holy Spirit. We might call Him the *Purity Spirit*. This Spirit, like oxygen, is something you can't see or touch, taste or smell, but you know when you have it and when you don't. And, as you genuinely follow steps 1 through 6, you can feel the Spirit of God at your core as He fills your void.

If you followed those steps of a deep cleanse to fill your void, then you automatically receive two amazing benefits:

1. By asking the Purity Spirit to "remain the core influencer of your core," you began an eternal relationship with God, your Heavenly Father (John 3:16). This eternal relationship ensures that, upon your physical death on earth, your core will transition into Heaven where you will abide forever with your Heavenly Father. In fact, you will even receive a new physical body in Heaven.

2. You've received the power of the *Purity Spirit* in your core. The *Purity Spirit* is

your source for discernment for every *decision you make in your purity driven life.* This is so important to understand. Many people cling to their faith, their knowledge of God, and religious rituals, but never tap into the source of God, the *Purity Spirit.* And thus, their void is never filled.

Don't neglect this new relationship with God. Allow the Spirit of God to fill the void in every area of your life.

"Daddy," a sad little voice inched around the corner of the department store aisle. And through my flooded eyes, my son, who was lost now stood before me. My broken and heavy heart leaped from my chest, as I ran towards Him and he jumped into my arms. "You're safe now, son. Daddy is here. I love you!"

Just like I never stopped looking for my son, our Heavenly Father has never stopped being in pursuit of you. Even in your darkest times and most distant places, lost and afraid, He's been calling out your name. **If you've asked Him to fill the *void* in your life,** He is telling you, "You're safe now, I am here now, son/daughter, and I love you."

Points to Ponder:

- *"I'm not ready to accept all that I've just read in this chapter to be true. I'm skeptical because:"*

- Or: *"I'm ready to fill my void with a deep cleanse:"* Write out your conversation to your Heavenly Father, following the steps 1 through 5 above:

NOTES:

FILLING MY VOID
IN EVERY AREA OF MY LIFE

We learned in the previous chapter that at the core of our heart we must have *purity* as the agent that influences the other four layers of our heart—and in turn, every decision we make. A *purity*-driven life is the only way to **daily** fill the God-Shaped Void within your heart.

Let's be honest, for some reading this book so far, the purity driven path makes perfect sense. Perhaps you've even taken the deep cleanse steps and a new peace and joy has birthed inside you, unlike anything you've ever experienced before.

Yet, for others reading this book, you just aren't sure yet. The Creation account in the Garden of Eden,

Easter story, talk of eternal life, and a purity spirit, just all seems too hard to fathom and you're skeptical. I understand. It is indeed a lot to digest. I encourage you to read the Bible verse references shown in the previous chapter. In the meantime, please read on. The *purity*-driven life is a universal truth application for every area of your life, not just spiritual. It relates to every decision you make.

After I spoke to an audience on this topic of living a purity-driven life, a lady in her mid-50's cornered me, "Hi Adam, I'm Nancy. Thanks for sharing tonight, but I have to be honest, I just don't get it, why is purity so important?"

I responded, "Nancy, I see a wedding ring on your hand. How long have you been married?"

A little taken back, she answered, "It will be 24 years next month. We were high school sweethearts," she added.

I smiled, "Well, you're certainly not in high school anymore, and so the ***premise*** that you were high school sweethearts really doesn't count for much 24 years later, but you're still in love, right?"

"Well yeah," She quipped.

"At that young age your husband probably *promised* you the moon when he asked you to marry him, right?"

"Yeah, he did," she said as she laughed.

"I'm guessing there are no spaceships in your driveway yet, but you don't mind, you still love him, right?"

"Of course!" she quickly answered.

She then went on to explain how romantic he was when they first met. How he would write her love notes and how attracted they were to each other. Then, she paused and admitted the *passion* in their marriage had dwindled. "But that is to be expected after all these years, but we still love each other. It's just different now, ya know?"

Perhaps feeling uncomfortable about her last statement, Nancy hurriedly shared, "We were young when we fell in love and we *purposefully* got married to have a family of our own." She paused. "But the kids never came. After several miscarriages we gave up trying."

"But you still love him after all these years, right?" I asked.

"Without a doubt; 100 percent," she assured me.

"So, let me recap, Nancy. Based on what you've shared, your marriage is no longer motivated by the *premise* of being high-school sweethearts, or the *promise* of the moon and stars, or the *passion* of two young lovers, or the *purpose* of raising a family. Those things are pretty much non-factors at this point right? But your marriage is still strong and you'll be celebrating your 24th anniversary soon right?"

"Oh yes!" her voice perked up.

I asked, "What if you came home tonight and found your husband in bed with another woman?"

Nancy's jaw dropped.

"What if you found out he had been having an affair with several women for many years? Would you still be celebrating that 24th anniversary?"

"Heck no!" Her voice intensified. "I'd throw him out of the house."

"So, you see, Nancy, your marriage can survive if it lacked any or all of these first four layers of core influencers, *premise, promises, passion, purpose,* but once the purity in your marriage is forfeited..."

"It's over!" Nancy finished my statement in agreement. "I get it now Adam. You're right. Nothing in our marriage matters if there isn't purity."

Yes, even a marriage overflowing with the influences of premise, promise, passion, and purpose isn't enough. A marriage without *purity* is unhealthy, with lethal ramifications leading to death of the love and the relationship fractured, often permanently broken.

The principle of a *purity*-driven life applies to *every* area of our lives.

Here is another practical example. Walk into a convenience store and you'll have options to quench your thirst with water. Evian is the most expensive, followed by Poland Spring, followed by the gas station brand. Each option offers the same *purpose*. Yet you can choose to pay for the brand you believe has the purest quality of taste.

There is a scene in the true story movie *Erin Brockovich* that explains this principle best. Erin is played by actress Julia Roberts. She and her legal team represent over 100 clients who have cancer because they claim the local chemical plant is polluting the water in their county. The power plant's legal representatives face off with them in a conference room showdown. The arrogant lady of the defense team states to Erin, "You have no proof the water is contaminated." She says this as she lifts a glass of water to her lips. Erin replies, "Go ahead and drink that water. We had it brought in special for you, straight from this county [where the chemical power plant is located]." A dramatic pause, then the defense attorney slowly places the glass of water down on the table without drinking it. Point made.

Even when compelled to reason or render a decision based on proof of *purpose* or *passionate* disdain we can never discount *purity*. The defense attorney had to pause and consider the *purity* of the water, even if she didn't want to.

I've heard and read lectures from hundreds of the most successful leaders from around the world. Probably 90% of them focus on *passion, purpose,* or process. Rarely do you hear the importance of a *purity*-driven leader. And yet all it takes is one *impure* personal or professional indiscretion or nefarious action to cause the entire fall of a leader on the highest pinnacle of success. Too often we learn of a pastor, a celebrity, or politician reaching their greatest *purpose* professionally, only to be disgraced publicly for their private *impurities*. It seems like every day we see on the news the latest fall from grace from someone who forfeited their *purity* in pursuit of their *passion, purpose,* and fulfillment.

What does it profit a man if he gains the whole world but forfeits his *purity*? (Matthew 16:26 & Mark 8:36)

Nestled in the valleys of central New York state is the rural town of Cooperstown. Its main street is lined with delis and stores, coffee shops, and hometown pizza parlors, reflecting an ambiance of generations come and gone. What makes this small, unassuming town a destination for millions of people every summer isn't the homemade food, the beautiful location, or the cooler weather, but rather the historic presence of the National Baseball Hall of Fame.

Every summer, baseball fans pour in to witness the enshrinement of players into the Baseball Hall of Fame.

The weekend festivities include a parade featuring current and former players. Along the street, hall-of-famers are sitting at tables on the sidewalk or inside storefronts selling their autographs. Many players will even sign or pose for pictures for free. I've met John Smoltz, Reggie Jackson, Johnny Bench, Harmon Killebrew, Yogi Berra, Phil Niekro, and Brooks Robinson, to name a few. It is a surreal experience to see so many of these baseball legends in person in a hometown atmosphere. As I stroll the sacred halls of the Baseball Hall of Fame, teaching my children about the history of the game, we see pictures and read statistics. But it saddens me every time when I think of what is missing. The greatest hitter of all time is nowhere mentioned or pictured.

Pete Rose retired in 1986, but has yet to be enshrined into the Hall of Fame. The Cincinnati Reds great set out to be the game's most successful player. The most important responsibility as a baseball player on offense is to get on base. Pete Rose did that better than anyone else. He got more hits than anyone in the history of the game before or since. He completed a career worthy of induction into the Hall of Fame, and yet he is forbidden.

Forbidden, because after his playing career, while serving as a coach, he broke a rule by betting on baseball games. Because of that, he was expelled from MLB (Major League Baseball). Not only has Pete Rose never been inducted as a member of the Hall of Fame, he is legally barred from being within 1,000 yards of the front doors of the Hall of Fame. For many years now, Pete Rose arrives in Cooperstown, sets up an autograph signing in a store front, as close to the HOF building as possible. It's a self-inflicting agony as he longs for the recognition that he worked so hard for... but which remains forbidden.

Pete Rose fulfilled his *purpose* becoming the greatest hitter the game has ever known. He played with an unmatched *passion*. As a player and coach he had enormous *power* of influence. His career gave him a life of *pleasure*. The *premise* remains today that he is still the greatest hitter ever to play the game. And yet, because he tainted the *purity* of the game, he has forfeited his legacy.

I don't know why Pete Rose chose to tarnish the game of baseball. Was there a *void* in his life that prompted such a reckless decision causing him to forfeit his legacy? If only he could go back in time and not make the same foolish choices. If only he could have seen then what his impure choice would cost him in his future. If only he had a decided to live *purity* driven.

There is no substitute for *purity* in our decision-making. No matter how strong the other four layers of influence are, they are pointless without *purity*.

The advertisement made the trip look *pleasurable*. The airplane ride *empowers* you to go anywhere in the world. When you booked your tickets you were *promised* a seat on the airplane. The flight crew was *passionate* about your timely arrival and departure. The flight route met the *purpose* of your trip. Although each of these core influencers are met, would you still get on the plane if you knew it wasn't safe? What if you saw the pilot drunk before loading the plane, would you still take the flight? If you were aware of something impure about the flight or airplane, you wouldn't choose to proceed.

The medical physician wants to restore your health so you can have the *pleasure* and the *empowerment* to live without pain. There is a *premise* that this is the best option of care for you. You are *promised* a specific diagnosis and plan of care. The doctors and nurses are *compassionate* about your needs. The *purpose* of your visit and pending surgery is clear. Yet, how important are those core influencers if the surgery, the facility, and the surgeon aren't safe?

In these examples we see the importance of purity—and how without it, the other four layers of our core influencers are rendered pointless.

Points to Ponder:

- *What other examples can you think of where legacies have been tarnished because of impure decisions?*

- *What impure decisions by others have negatively impacted your life, as a child, as an adult?*

- *What impurities are you tempted with today or already struggling with?*

- *How might these impurities impact your life today and in the future?*

NOTES:

10

STRATEGIC **PAUSE**

Through the first eight chapters, you've learned what the five core layers are. You've discovered the secret to what needs to be at the center of your core. Now how do we daily apply this knowledge to keep our lives free of *void*?

The first step is to practice, with every decision, asking yourself, "Am I making this decision from the center of my core or from a surface or outer ring influencer?" The key to living a consistent void-free life is to practice making a **STRATEGIC PAUSE** to align your core decision making. Make an intentional effort to practice strategic pauses. Some pauses may last a few seconds; other strategic pauses may last days or even weeks as you intentionally seek the discernment of what a *pure* decision actually is.

Take the following example of a strategic pause:

It was the mid 1980's when David and his sister Michelle were teenagers. Their father was a very successful leader in a food manufacturing company. Packaging food products was his forte. He was the person who invented microwavable soups. One evening, the family stopped at a popular fast-food restaurant for dinner. David's mouth watered with great *pleasure* as he saw the picture of a bucket of chicken on the menu sign. The family chose this restaurant under the *premise* that it was their favorite place to eat. The fast-food brand *promised* the best-tasting chicken anywhere! The family sat down at the table with a fresh bucket of warm fried chicken at the center. David could hardly control his *passion* to dive in and claim the first chicken wing. He gave a very quick prayer of blessing over the food while simultaneously reaching towards the bucket. "Wait!" his dad demanded loudly. "But Dad, we already prayed and washed our hands and..." C'mon Dad, we are hungry," his daughter also chimed in. "Honey, the kids are starving," his wife said, reminding him of the *purpose* of their visit to feed their hunger quickly rather than going home to cook a meal. The father sat quietly and gazed intently at the bucket of chicken, becoming fixated on the meal before them. The kids looked at each other, then at their mom. "What's wrong with Dad?" David asked. At that moment the father methodically stretched out his arm and reached towards the top of the bucket and in slow motion pulled out a warm, crispy, brown...rat. Somehow a rat had ended up in the basket of chicken that got fried and served up for dinner. Imagine what would have happened without the *strategic pause* before making a simple decision to begin eating.

And so, I ask you, in this decision, what was the most important influencer, the *pleasurable* appetite, the *premise* and *promise* of quality food, a *passionate* and *purposeful* hunger, or the *purity* of the meal itself? Suppose for a moment that the father didn't take the *strategic pause*, and the other four core influencers prompted them to eat dinner, not knowing they were eating fried rat instead of fried chicken. Imagine the consequences of not making a *purity*-driven decision:

the immediate sickness, possible long-term illness, the emotional trauma, the legal lawsuit that might ensue. That doesn't include the nightmare for the restaurant owners.

How many decisions, great and small, do we make daily that leave us sick, with disfigured and traumatized lives that could have been avoided had we only taken a *strategic pause*?

A strategic pause is literally refraining from responding or acting upon a choice for a moment, however brief or long, to ensure you make the healthiest choice possible.

Three steps of a strategic pause in decision-making:

1. Retreat: Don't respond or act upon a decision. Step back and take the necessary time for introspection rather than impulse thinking.
2. Recognize: Which of the five layers of my core is most strongly influencing my decision right now? Does this decision violate my values based on my center core influencer of *purity*? What is the

healthiest option? Never compromise purity in the name of *purpose, pleasure,* or any of the other core influencers.

3. Resume: Make your decision from a *pure* heart of discernment.

Retreat, Recognize and Resume. Say those three a few times out loud and memorize them.

The easiest way to remember and implement a strategic pause is by letting **inspection rule over impulse** every time! Live introspectively rather than impulsively. This requires self-control and consistent practice.

President Dwight D. Eisenhower practiced a strategic pause called "The 24-Hour Rule." Whenever he wrote a letter in response to a difficult situation, he would put it in the drawer of his office desk and wait 24 hours before mailing it. This strategic pause ensured that he took enough time to make sure his response was warranted. At the end of his presidency, his desk was full of un-mailed letters.

I realize that for many of us, the strategic pause in the decision-making process is not always that simple when we are faced with tough life decisions—especially if we are handicapped by addictions, PTSD, a history of trauma, or simply a lack of the knowledge needed to make an informed decision on a given subject. Hardship can stop at anyone's door at any time. And when it does, we aren't always equipped to handle it in the moment. But even in the deepest, darkest trenches of a massive *void*, there is hope.

When Jesus died on the cross to pay the penalty for humanity's *void*, the restoration plan did not stop there. Easter happened. Three days after Jesus's body was removed from the wooden instrument of his execution, wrapped in a cloth, and placed in a tomb, Jesus came back to life and literally walked out of the tomb. He was seen by many people before he ascended into heaven. In His place, God provided an essence of His likeness that is called the Holy Spirit. We might call Him the *Purity Spirit*. If you followed those steps in Chapter 6 to fill your void by beginning a relationship with God, then you automatically received the *power* of the *Purity Spirit* in your core. The *Purity Spirit* is your source for discernment for every *strategic pause*.

If we rely on our own ability, we are going to make mistakes. We will lack the discernment, will-power, and self-control to choose the purity driven-decision. I remind myself daily of these bookend truths of the Bible: Apart from God we will fail, but through God all things are possible.

Through God's Spirit dwelling within our core, we have the capacity to live a life of meaning and fulfillment, free of void. There is no void too deep for God to pull us out of, if we're only willing to ask.

Points to Ponder:

- *In what areas of your life will it be the hardest to practice a strategic pause?*

- *What are examples of times you wish you had taken a strategic pause but didn't? What was the consequence?*

- *What are the decisions you are facing right now for which you need to retreat, recognize and resume with a strategic pause, asking God for discernment?*

NOTES:

RELATIONSHIP, **NOT RELIGION**

The essence of the true meaning of life is to know and love God, period. Nothing more. Nothing less than that. Does that mean nothing else matters? No, there are many things that contribute to our happiness and comfort. But nothing can substitute for a genuine relationship with God.

God is far less concerned with how we earn our paycheck, whether we marry a blonde or a brunette, if we live in the north or the south, if we get a parking space up front or in the back, if our favorite sports team wins the championship or not.

He did not offer Himself up as a sacrifice on a cross so that He would be our personal genie and grant us a *purpose*-filled life with a basket full of wishes and blessings. In fact, contrary to popular religious leaders, God doesn't even promise financial prosperity, good health, popularity, or protection from natural disasters.

He gave, lived, died, resurrected, forgave, restored, and loves you and me because He wants to have an eternal personal relationship with each of us. A relationship that extends far beyond our limited time on earth.

Spend your days seeking Him, spending time with Him in your own garden or special meeting place. Make Him your focus rather than an endless quest for purpose. I realize that last statement doesn't sell books. It's also why I didn't title this book, *The Purity-Driven Life*, because let's be honest: you wouldn't have opened it. The market is flooded with books and resources about blessings, favor, and prosperity. "A purity-driven" life doesn't sound as appealing as having a "life of abundance," that so many preachers, high-profile authors and celebrity Christians try to sell us.

(Here is a free bonus tip worth remembering: Any time money is mentioned as a requirement or channel to your "finding fulfillment" or a "life of blessings," run the other way! It's not true. It is impossible to buy or spend our way to authentic lasting fulfillment. [John 2:13-16])

God didn't create us to have a laundry list of purposes. He created us to know and love Him. God does bless. He does shine favor upon us. However, it is all done in proportion to our relationship with Him, determined by His grace, mercy, and love and not of ourselves.

That is hard for some of us to digest. Many of us have grown up in a Christianity that preaches *purpose* as the climax of our aspirations, the foundation of our faith. We've based everything on this quest to discover and define our purpose in order that we might be fulfilled, when all along God was just asking, "Where are you? Do you love Me? Will you spend time with Me?"

Our existence starts there. Our core starts with the God-shaped void that only He Himself can fill. Not our job or our ministry, not our relationships, not our successes, and not even our religiousness. Only truly knowing God and having intimate fellowship with Him will satisfy our void daily, hourly, moment by moment.

RELATIONSHIP, NOT RELIGION

How long have you hid from him? What have you clothed yourself with? What are you unsuccessfully filling your void with?

Author Sammy Tippet in his book titled *Fire in Your Heart* states that most of us "live lives of convenience and complacency rather than character and commitment." A purity-driven life is all about consistent integrity.

Conviction is the gatekeeper of character and commitment. I don't mean "conviction" as a legal term here. Conviction is an inner voice of discernment and commitment. Conviction is made possible by an incredible gift given to us by God our Heavenly Father, called the Holy Spirit. When you say "yes" to filling the God-shaped void with His forgiveness, grace, and love, you automatically receive the gift of the Holy Spirit indwelling within you. This is the essence that drives all five of your core influencers. More importantly, the Holy Spirit allows you to have a relationship with God. This relationship is an unbreakable union between you and your Heavenly Father. When you talk to God, it is His Holy Spirit that responds back by communicating directly in and through your core.

Points to Ponder:

- *Describe moments in your life when you felt the conviction of the Holy Spirit.*

- *What are some examples you've seen in others or in your own life where being religious became more important than having a genuine relationship with God?*

NOTES:

12

GRACE, **NOT LEGALISM**

Caution: The purity-driven life is not a life governed by rules and regulations. It is not a license for others to judge you or measure your character by your purity. Within the Christian religious sector, there are whole denominations designed to control, manipulate, and brainwash followers through incorrect theology. These groups of people misrepresent the life and teachings of Jesus in the name of *power*. They manipulate through fear and false teachings. They subscribe their followers to a life of rule keeping in the name of religion. This is called legalism.

Legalism is best described as manmade rules of living a Christian life.

Through strict and sterile boundaries, they form a wall between them and "the world" around them. They distort Bible verses and create unfounded lifestyle parameters to control their members.

I first experienced legalism as a teenager singing in a Christian talent contest. I was disqualified because my hair was over my collar, and the Christian ballad I sang had a drum beat. And according to these self-anointed spiritual leaders, those were grounds for not looking "Christian" enough.

I also lived in a community where the First Baptist Church refused to have a joint picnic with Calvary Baptist Church just one mile up the road, because they were not identical in their theology.

My friend Terry stayed in an abusive marriage for decades because she was taught in her church that "divorce was a sin." She finally got the courage to leave when the abuse nearly killed her. Even after leaving, she was condemned with shame for "divorcing" her husband. This kind of unhealthy *power* used in the name of Christianity is perverted and impure.

The tenets of the Christian faith can be a source of

instruction, with the Bible being a guide for developing spiritual maturity. The danger becomes when these resources are structured and imposed in such a way that they violate the very freedom Jesus came to give us. Authority and accountability imposed by religious leaders and groups can often become legalistic.

Your purity-driven life is subject to God and His Spirit leading you, and not fodder for others to condemn or manipulate you.

It's been said that "whenever you mix legalism with grace, it distorts grace and makes a mockery of the cross."

Even in His lifetime, Jesus stood up against legalism and the religious people who manipulated others for their selfish purposes, their hunger for *power*, and their personal *pleasure*. The Pharisees were one of the most vocal and influential religious societies of Jesus' time on earth. The word *Pharisee* is a Hebrew word meaning "separatists, or separated ones." They opposed Jesus and His teachings because He did not conform to their legalism. Jesus accused them of hypocrisy and pretentiousness.

The lesson we learn from Jesus' interaction with legalism is to never substitute relationship for religion. We must caution ourselves from allowing the purposes of religion to take precedence over *purity* of relationship with God. Like so many religious leaders of today, the irony of the Pharisees is that they were so devoted to their religious law-keeping that they were blind to the very presence of God in their midst. May we never become so addicted to rule-keeping and religious practices that we miss the very essence of God's presence in our daily lives!

Points to Ponder:

- *The Pharisee's passion and purposes eventually led them to having Jesus killed. In what subtle or extreme ways has legalism or religious imposters impacted your life?*

- *In what ways has the grace of God set you free from legalism in your own life?*

NOTES:

13

LIVING THE LIFE
YOU WERE CREATED FOR

Living a purity-driven life is not easy. A battle rages within every one of us: our impure human nature against the Spirit of God, and the Spirit of God against our impure human nature. (Galatians 5:7). Living a selfless existence marked by humility, compassion, frugality, and servant leadership is counterintuitive and counter-cultural. We live in a self-absorbed, materialistic, fast-paced, instant gratification world. And just like Adam and Eve were deceived in the Garden of Eden, by questioning the *purpose* of God's instruction to them, and thus blinding them to the *purity* of the temptation before them, so too will you and I be faced with deceptive lies. For us to deny the presence of impurity and disobedience in our life is self-deception (1 John 1:8).

Therefore, we must always remember that moral lapses are not simply mistakes in judgment, but are impurities against a Holy God (Psalm 51:4). To be pure in heart one must confess **all** impurities and mistakes to God and forsake them utterly, reestablishing our relationship with Him (1 John 1:9).

We cannot pick and choose which areas of our life to remain pure while other areas are impure. A *purity-driven life* means doing **all** that is wholesome, ethical, morally right, spiritually healthy, and Biblically sound, by keeping ourselves in the love of God (Jude 21).

A transformation of character always begins with our core. In Scriptural imagery, the heart represents our core inner life. When people today speak figuratively of the heart, they refer only to the emotions or feelings. But in the Bible, the meaning is much broader. The heart is represented as the center of our being, our core. It is the source of our thoughts, feelings, decisions and conduct, both good and bad.

Jesus said, "A good man, out of the good treasure of the heart, brings forth good things, and an evil man, out of the evil treasure, brings forth evil things" (Matthew 12:35). All human behavior issues stem from the heart, our *core*.

Jesus requires us to have a *core* free of duplicity and pretense. He spoke of an eye that is "single" or focused upon what is true and righteous (Matthew 6:22). That is, without mixed motives or a hidden agenda.

Those who would be *pure* in heart must strive to live in constant resistance of *every* evil thought, motive, and desire that arises from within.

If you let Him, over the next few hours, days, weeks, months, and years, the Holy Spirit is going to do a redefining of your core and align your five influencers. Perfection does not lie ahead. Struggle will still greet you. Pain, pride, and other possibilities will attack your purity. But still the Holy Spirit will remain as your source to guide you and strengthen you in your purity-driven life—if you allow Him. God has given us everything we need to live a purity-driven life and fill the void in our life, by His divine power. (2 Peter 1:3)

Make this verse from Psalm 51:10 a daily prayer: "Spirit of the living God, fall afresh on me. Create in me a clean heart, God, and renew a steadfast spirit within."

Make these two attributes a daily practice:
- **Deep Cleansing**
- **Strategic Pauses**

As a result, you'll develop the discipline and maturity to channel every decision from the innermost layer of your core, while still giving value to the other four layers. Thus ensuring the healthiest option for the best possible outcome.

We make on average 20,000 decisions every day of our lives. Imagine if they were all purity-driven decisions! How much different would our lives be then? Unfortunately, we are going to make mistakes. We aren't always going to get it right. But what if we could make 10% of our decisions from a foundation of purity? Perhaps 25%? And, eventually, we could make the majority of our decisions purity-driven ones.

Where do I start? Here is a simple exercise that you can begin today. Look back at the end of your day and write down just one word that represents a decision you made (big or small). Then, write down as many words/decisions you can remember. Next, looking at the Core Decision-Making Model, decide what core influencer prompted your decision. Then, evaluate how might the outcome have been different if you had made the decision from a foundation of "is there anything impure (potentially unhealthy)" about this decision? What are the possible negative consequences of my choice? Applying the purity-driven life principle will become second nature to you as you retrain your core by practicing strategic pauses and allowing the Spirit of God to lead you.

In conclusion, The **Core Decision-Making Model** is the compass for addressing your *God-Shaped Void*. **Purity** reveals **purpose**. Your **purpose** is fueled by your **passion**. Your **passion** produces a healthy **premise** and **promises**. From these premises and promises you are **empowered** to make the best decisions leading to **pleasure** and or satisfaction. As you are **purity**-driven in your decision-making, you will experience the fulfilling life you were created for.

Points to Ponder:

- *Imagine a world where every culture practiced purity-driven-living. How would it look different?*

  Purity-driven leadership...
  Purity-driven marriage...
  Purity-driven politics...
  Purity-driven businesses...
  Purity-driven conversations...
  Purity-driven eating...
  Purity-driven thinking...
  Purity-driven _____

- *What areas in your life do you most desire to see this purity principle applied?*

- *How has this book changed the way you will live your life moving forward?*

- *How will you lead differently in your home, in your work, in your community?*

NOTES:

For additional resources, products and blog visit:
GodShapedVoid.com

Now available: *God-Shaped Void* music CD with songs inspired by the book.

Like the *God-Shaped Void* Facebook page.